First Steps in Single-Session Therapy

I0102992

By the same author
and published by Rationality Publications

*When Time Is at a Premium: Cognitive-Behavioural Approaches to
Single-Session Therapy and Very Brief Coaching* (2016)
*Attitudes in Rational Emotive Behaviour Therapy (REBT):
Components, Characteristics and Adversity-Related
Consequences* (2016)
Windy Dryden Live! (2021)
Windy Dryden Collected! (2022)
*The REBT Pocket Companion for Clients, 2nd Edition
(with Walter J. Matweychuk)* (2022)
The Little Book of Therapeutic Rationality (2022)
*Thought for the Day: A Flexible Approach to
Mental Health* (2022)
*Seizing Moments and Being Useful: The Development of a Single-
Session Therapist* (2025)
WWW: The Collected Wonderful Words of Windy (2025)

'Seven Principles' Series

Seven Principles of Good Mental Health (2021)
Seven Principles of Rational Emotive Behaviour Therapy (2021)
Seven Principles of Single-Session Therapy (2021)
Seven Principles of Doing Live Therapy Demonstrations (2021)

'First Steps' Series

*First Steps in Rational Emotive Behaviour Therapy: A Guide to
Practising REBT in Peer Counselling, 2nd Edition* (2025)
First Steps in Rational Emotive Behaviour Therapy for Clients (2025)
*First Steps in Using Rational Emotive Behaviour Therapy in
Coaching* (2025)
First Steps in Single-Session Therapy (2025)

First Steps in Single-Session Therapy

When Clients Want Help with Specific Problems

Windy Dryden

Rationality Publications

Rationality Publications
136 Montagu Mansions, London W1U 6LQ

www.rationalitypublications.com
info@rationalitypublications.com

Copyright (c) 2025 Windy Dryden

The right of Windy Dryden to be identified as the author of this work
has been asserted in accordance with sections 77 and 78 of the
Copyright Designs and Patents Act 1988.

A catalogue record of this book is
available from the British Library.

First edition 2025

Condition of sale:
This book is sold subject to the condition that it shall not, by way of
trade or otherwise, be lent, sold or hired out or otherwise circulated in
any form of binding or cover other than that in which it is published
and without a similar condition including this condition being
imposed on the subsequent purchaser.

ISBN: 978-1-914938-45-0

Contents

Preface   7

What is Single-Session Therapy? A Brief Introduction   9

Part 1   SST: The Pre-Conversation Phase   15
Step 1   Set Up Your Practice and Disseminate   17
Step 2   Adopt a Single-Session Therapy Mindset to Help
         Your Client with a Specific Problem   20

Part 2: SST: The Beginning Phase   25
Step 3   Respond to the First Contact from the Person   27
Step 4   Contract with Your Client   28
Step 5   Invite Your Client to Prepare for the Conversation   31
Step 6   Invite Your Client to Nominate a Problem   33
Step 7   Elicit a Conversation Goal from Your Client   35
Step 8   Agree on a Focus with Your Client, Stay Focused
         and Periodically Check that the Focus is Still Relevant   38
Step 9   Help Yourself and Your Client to Understand Their
         Nominated Problem and a Problem-Related Goal   41

Part 3   SST The Middle Phase   47
Step 10 Enquire about Your Client's Past Attempts to Deal
         with the Nominated Problem and Other Problems   49
Step 11 Forage for Internal and External Resources   51
Step 12 Elicit Your Client's Views on How to Solve Their
         Problem   55
Step 13 Offer Your 'Take' to Your Client   58
Step 14 Help Your Client to Construct a Solution   60

Step 15 Invite Your Client to Rehearse Their Constructed
Solution   64
Step 16 Develop an Implementation Plan with Your Client and
Identify and Deal with Obstacles to Implementation   67

Part 4   The Ending Phase and Beyond   69
Step 17 Invite Your Client to Summarise the Conversation   71
Step 18 Elicit Your Client's Takeaways   73
Step 19 Encourage Your Client to Generalise Their Learning   74
Step 20 Discuss How Your Client May Access Further Help   75
Step 21 Deal with any Unfinished Business with Your Client   77
Step 22 Seek Immediate Feedback from Your Client   79
Step 23 Seek Longer-Term Feedback from Your Client   81

Appendix 1   84
Appendix 2   86
Appendix 3   88
Appendix 4   90
References   93
Index   95

Preface

Single-session therapy is a mode of delivering therapy services where the intention is to help the client achieve what they have come for from that conversation and where both therapist and client understand that the client can access more help once they have gotten all they can from the conversation. Thus, it is not 'one shot' therapy or 'one and done' therapy, although if the client states in advance that they only want to come once, the therapist respects their decision.

What does the word 'session' mean in single-session therapy? In my view, a 'session' has three components: (a) the preparation that the client does for the conversation that they will have with you, (b) the conversation itself, and (c) the work that your client does after the conversation before deciding whether or not they need further help.

Single-session therapy thrives in an environment where help is provided to the client at the point when the client requests it and not at the point of appointment availability. This is why, in my view, the best context for SST is in 'open-access, enter now' services where the client can come into a centre and be seen on that visit with minimal wait.

Clients come to SST with different preferences concerning how they want to be helped by the therapist, although they may find it difficult to articulate them without the therapist's help. Thus, a person may come to SST hoping to (i) explore a particular issue, (ii) understand their problem better, (iii) be heard and understood, (iv) get matters off their chest, (v) make a decision, (vi) resolve a dilemma or (vii) discuss how they may best address their problem in a more extended manner. However, the most common form of help clients seek from SST is to solve a particular emotional or behavioural problem with which they have become stuck (Dryden, 2025). Consequently, this book is devoted to single-session therapy, where clients seek solution-focused help for their specific problems.

In this book, I will outline 23 steps you can take to help your client with their specific problem. These steps are divided into four parts: (1) the pre-conversation phase, (2) the beginning phase, (3) the middle phase and (4) the ending phase and beyond. While I have presented these steps logically, I do not suggest you follow them in this order. The best way to use these steps is to view them like a handy person views their tools in a toolbox. They won't use all these tools but know where they are if needed.

No book can give you all you need to become a single-session therapist. There is no substitute for training, experience and supervision from those who are themselves experienced in SST. However, this book can help your development as an SST therapist and is best used as an overarching framework for the work.

Windy Dryden
London & Eastbourne, December 2024

What is Single-Session Therapy?
A Brief Introduction

The Nature of Single-Session Therapy

Single-session therapy (SST) can be defined as 'an intentional form of helping where you and your client[1] contract to have a conversation, during which you both work together to you're your client take away what they have come for. This is based on the knowledge that your client can have more help later if they want it'. This conversation can be face-to-face, online or text-based. Here, the communication is synchronous.[2] Its main features are that it is interactive and that the communications between you and your client can immediately influence each other. It is generally agreed that, ideally, your client should not be offered more help at the end of the conversation. This is because the full impact of the conversation on your client can only be gauged by them when they have had an opportunity to (a) reflect on what they have taken from the conversation, (b) digest this learning to determine its applicability, (c) put this learning into practice and (d) see the effect of doing so. Only then can they see with clarity whether they require further help.

It is important that you and your client agree upon the latter's goals for the conversation and that you offer your client the help

---

[1] By client, in this book, I mean an individual, although SST can also be practised with couples or families.
[2] Synchronous communication involves you and your client communicating in real time. Asynchronous communication involves a therapist and client communicating where there is a delay between when a message is sent and when the other person receives, interprets it and then replies. For the purposes of this book, I do not consider asynchronous communication in therapy to be single-session therapy.

that they are seeking.[3] It is generally believed that single-session therapy is solution-focused in nature, and as I mentioned in the preface, the scope of this book is SST for clients seeking help for specific problems.

The Single-Session Therapy Mindset

The effective practice of single-session therapy occurs when your work is founded on a single-session therapy mindset[4] as opposed to what might be called a conventional therapy mindset.[5]

In this section, I will outline the main features of the single-session therapy mindset.[6]

One Conversation or More, Be Open to Both Possibilities

In SST, you should approach the conversation thinking that while this may be the only time that you will see your client, the latter may seek more help later. You should not approach the conversation thinking that it will be the first of several or more conversations or that SST means one conversation and one conversation only.

---

[3] The likelihood of a good outcome in SST is enhanced when goal congruence (Cooper & Law, 2018) and help congruence (Norcross & Cooper, 2021) are both present.

[4] Some SST therapists refer to this as single-session thinking (see Hoyt, Young and Rycroft, 2021).

[5] For a discussion of the differences between these two mindsets, see Dryden (2023).

[6] For a more complete discussion of the single-session therapy mindset, see Cannistrà (2022).

It Is Possible to Start Therapy from the First Moment and Without Prior Knowledge of the Person

Conventional therapy usually begins with a period of assessment where the client is assessed for their suitability for therapy. If deemed suitable, the assessor determines the type of therapy that is best suited for their problems and how much therapy they should be offered. In this approach, therapy begins once this assessment has been concluded. By contrast, in SST, therapy begins without you having prior knowledge of the person. Here, assessment is seen to delay the beginning of therapy, which commences immediately. If necessary, you can ask your client what they think you need to know about them in order to help them.

Potentially, Anyone Can Be Helped in a Single Conversation, but This Does Not Mean that Everyone Will Be Helped in a Single Conversation

As a single-session therapist you consider that everybody is deemed suitable for SST and you proceed on this basis.[7] Your client judges whether they have benefitted from the conversation after they have had it and have engaged in the reflect-digest-act-decide process described earlier. However, just because anyone can be helped in a single conversation does not mean everyone will be helped. If your client is not helped, you both determine a way forward for them. In conclusion, the best way of determining if your client will benefit from SST is for them to have the conversation with you and see if they benefit later.

---

[7] Here, I assume that your client has given their informed consent to proceed.

SST Is Client-Led

SST is focused on what your client wants. They get to choose the focus of the conversation and what they want to achieve from it. They also get to choose how much therapy they want. If you have concerns about any of these issues, you should voice them and discuss them openly with your client.

The Therapist Is Transparent

Following on from the above, you are transparent with your client. You are clear about what SST is and what it is not, and what you can and can't do.

Focus on What Is Right with the Client, Not What Is Wrong with Them

While you are aware that your client is seeking help for a problem, you are keen to help them identify how they can apply their previous relevant successful problem-solving efforts to this problem. In doing so, you encourage your client to identify and utilise their internal and external resources. The focus is on what is right with the person, not what is wrong with them.

The Conversation Is Tailored to the Client. The Client Is Not Tailored to the Therapist's Preferred Approach

SST is bespoke therapy. Thus, you strive to tailor the therapy to your client rather than fit the client to the therapy. Consequently, most SST therapists do not claim to practise a specific approach to SST, although they may be, at times, informed by ideas that stem from their favoured therapeutic orientation(s).

The Client–Therapist Relationship Can Be Established Rapidly

The therapeutic alliance can be established quickly (see Dryden, 2024). This is done by identifying and helping your client meet their goal from the conversation, providing them with the help that they seek, and forming a good working bond. When this is done, a good therapeutic outcome tends to occur (Simon, Imel, Ludman & Steinfeld, 2012).

Part 1

SST: The Pre-Conversation Phase

STEP 1

Set Up Your Practice and Disseminate

If a gardener wants a plant to flourish in their garden, they need to prepare the soil first. This involves them doing two things. First, they must remove any weeds, rocks and debris from the soil. Second, they must ensure the plant receives sufficient water, oxygen and other nutrients to flourish. If the gardener ignores this principle and plants the seed without adequately preparing the soil, the plant will not flourish; it will soon wither.

The same is true with your single-session therapy practice. You need to remove obstacles to the flourishing of this practice and ensure the presence of several facilitative conditions.

Be Committed to Providing Help at the Point of Need

As I pointed out in the Preface, single-session therapy thrives in a practice built on offering help at the point of need rather than at the point of appointment availability. If you are a therapist in independent practice and it is not practicable for you to establish an 'open-access, enter now' service[8], then you may consider devoting specific times in your working week to offering clients SST appointments. In my view, if a person has to wait longer than one week for a single-session therapy appointment, then the potency of SST begins to drain away.

If you work in an agency, then it is again best if SST is established on the 'help at the point of need' principle. Many

---

[8] Such a service used to be called 'walk-in'. The name was changed because it was thought that the term 'walk-in' would be unwelcoming to people who cannot walk.

clinical managers are attracted to SST as a way of reducing waiting lists and waiting times for clients. While this is understandable, this is not the purpose of SST. Its purpose is to offer people prompt help for an issue troubling them and who don't want to commit to several sessions to get that help. That said, once SST is introduced into an agency, the consequence is a reduction in waiting lists and waiting times.

Assess Problems, Not People

Many therapists, both in independent practice and in agencies, use the first psychotherapy session to assess the client. This involves collecting a lot of data which, from the perspective of single-session therapy, is largely unnecessary. This is particularly the case when it comes to assessing a person for their suitability for SST. There are two reasons why it is important for you to refrain from this practice. First, the best way of determining whether a person will benefit from SST is to offer them SST to see if they benefit. In other words, there are no valid criteria that you can use to gauge client suitability for SST reliably. Second, if you assess for client suitability, you are violating a cardinal principle of SST: offer therapy immediately.

By all means, assess the client's nominated[9] problem during the conversation, but refrain from doing any other form of assessment. There is one rider to this. You may work in an agency that mandates all its therapists when they see clients for the first time to collect data for funders and to assess client risk. In this case, you must comply with this practice. However, after you have done so, begin the conversation. In this case, this will be longer than usual. Here, it is important to explain to your client what you have to do before helping them with their nominated problem.

---

[9] I refer to the problem that the client wants help with as their 'nominated' problem.

Disseminate Your Service to Potential Clients and Stakeholders

Once you or the agency in which you work decide to offer SST as part of what is available to potential clients, then it is crucial that this service be disseminated clearly to this group and other relevant stakeholders (such as funders and referrers). This is done by having meetings to explain SST and respond to any doubts, reservations and objections these groups may have about SST. SST needs to be clearly explained on your website and, if relevant, that of the agency in which you work.

Client Choice

The aim of such dissemination material is to enable clients to understand SST and make an informed choice concerning whether to access it. It is important to stress that no client should be compelled to have SST when they don't want it. In addition, when clients are offered a choice of different modes of therapy delivery, their choice concerning which mode best suits their current circumstance is paramount and should be accepted unless there is a good reason not to do so. This reason should be explained to the client and discussed with them.

STEP 2

Adopt a Single-Session Therapy Mindset to Help Your Client with a Specific Problem

Different modes of therapy delivery are practised best when the therapist holds the most relevant mindset to that work. If you bring a mindset that is inappropriate to a particular way of practising therapy, the result is usually counterproductive. Imagine, for example, bringing a single-session therapy mindset to psychoanalysis and vice versa.

In the opening section to this book, entitled, 'What is Single-Session Therapy? A Brief Introduction', I discussed important elements of the single-session therapy mindset.[10] These are:

- One Conversation or More, Be Open to Both Possibilities
- It is Possible to Start Therapy from the First Moment and Without Prior Knowledge of the Person
- Potentially, Anyone Can Be Helped in a Single Conversation, but This Does Not Mean that Everyone Will Be Helped in a Single Conversation
- SST Is Client-Led
- The Therapist Is Transparent
- Focus on What Is Right with the Client, Not What Is Wrong with Them
- The Conversation Is Tailored to the Client. The Client Is Not Tailored to the Therapist's Preferred Approach
- The Client–Therapist Relationship Can Be Established Rapidly

---

[10] See that section for a discussion of these elements.

The SST Mindset with Special Reference to Helping Clients with Their Specific Problems

In addition to the elements of the single-session mindset listed above, the following additional elements of this mindset are particularly relevant to helping your client with their nominated specific problem.

Be Problem-Focused from the Outset

Productive use of time in single-session therapy is paramount; therefore, it is important to remember that a very early focus on the problem that your client wishes to discuss with you is vital.

Agree on Your Client's Nominated Problem

Sometimes, your client may have several problems they may wish to discuss with you in SST, but you don't have time to do this. If you attempt to do so, you will probably end up not helping them with any of their problems. So, remember the importance of helping your client select the most important problem for them to address at that time. As I have already said, I call this problem the 'nominated' problem.

Keep in Mind the Importance of Negotiating an End-of-Conversation Goal with Your Client

It is important to keep in mind that this may be the only time you have to help your client with their nominated problem. As such, it is important that you be forward-looking and help your client set an end-of-conversation goal. This goal will provide a direction for the remainder of the conversation.

Keep in Mind the Importance of Co-Creating a Therapeutic Focus and Maintaining It Once It Has Been Created

The client's nominated problem and the end-of-conversation goal should provide the focus for the conversation. Keep this in mind and agree on this focus with your client. Once the focus is agreed upon, remember to maintain it.

When Your Client Speaks Their Nominated Problem Out Loud, Doing So Sometimes Helps Them to Find a Solution

If your client has not had an opportunity to tell another person about their nominated problem, the very act of speaking this out loud may be beneficial in helping them find a solution later in the session. This value of the act of speaking out loud should not be underestimated.

Sometimes, Helping Your Client to Understand Their Problem Is All that Is Needed

Similarly, once you have helped your client to understand their problem, that may be all that is needed, their new understanding suggesting a solution to them that they can implement later.

Build on What the Client Has Done Before to Address Their Nominated Problem

Your client may have made numerous attempts to solve their nominated problem. Keep this in mind and discover what they are. Remember to build on their helpful attempts as you work towards constructing a solution with them.

You May Not Be Able to Help Your Client Solve Their Problem in One Session, but You Can Equip Them with a Solution for Later Application

In many cases, the best you can do with your client in a single conversation is to help them (a) select a solution to their nominated problem, (b) rehearse it during the conversation and (c) plan to implement the solution in their everyday life.

Helping Your Client Reframe Their Problem May Be All that Is Needed

Perhaps the only time a client will leave the conversation thinking that their problem has been solved is when you have helped them reframe it so that it is no longer a problem. Think of this as you work with them to develop a solution to their nominated problem.

Helping Your Client Take an Initial Step in the Right Direction May Encourage Them to Take Additional Constructive Steps Later

It is important that you are realistic about what can be achieved from a single conversation when your client needs to implement their selected solution after the session. Here, 'small is often beautiful', and helping your client to take an initial step to solve their problem may be important in encouraging them to take additional steps later.

A Complex Problem May Not Require a Complex Solution

It is often thought that clients need a complex solution if they have a complex problem. However, therapists who work in 'open-access, enter now' services report that it is possible to help a client with a complex problem in a single conversation by encouraging them to get to the heart of the issue. Doing so will help you and your client to develop a do-able solution to their problem.

Part 2

SST: The Beginning Phase

STEP 3

Respond to the First Contact

I have found it useful to think of a person occupying one of two roles when they contact me for the first time: the 'enquirer' role or the 'applicant' role. When they occupy the role of 'enquirer', they contact me to ask therapeutic-related questions about SST (e.g. 'What exactly is single-session therapy?' 'Can I have more than one session?') or practical questions about SST (e.g. 'How quickly can I be seen?' or How much does the therapy cost?'). In general, I am happy to answer such questions. I am aware, however, that they may be contacting other therapists and agencies about SST or other therapy delivery modes.

When an 'enquirer' asks me questions and it is clear that they do not know much about single-session therapy, then I will refer them to the description of single-session therapy on my website or send them an information sheet that I developed on SST (see Appendix 1).

When an 'applicant' makes contact with me they have concluded that they want to have SST and want to make an appointment to see me. When this happens, I send them a contract to sign, which outlines the practicalities of seeing me. I generally conclude that they know about SST. However, if I think the person would benefit from knowing more about SST before I accept their application, I send them the description of SST presented in Appendix 1.

When an agency provides SST, it may be difficult for potential clients to make contact and ask questions that are important to them. This is particularly the case when contacts are largely online. In this circumstance, therapists may need to take particular care that clients have understood the nature of SST and what it can and can't do before they proceed with SST (see Step 4).

STEP 4

Contract with Your Client

Like all other modes of therapy delivery, single-session therapy is based on the ethical principle of informed consent. This means that your client needs to be informed about SST, demonstrate an accurate understanding of SST and then consent to go forward based on this understanding.

What Constitutes a Contract in SST

Consenting to SST means that your client understands that:

1. You and they will work together to help the client leave the conversation that you have had with them with what they have come for. In the context of this book, this means leaving the conversation with a solution to their nominated problem and with a plan to implement it afterwards.
2. They will go away from the conversation and do the following:

   - They will reflect on what they have learned from the conversation
   - They will digest their learning and see how they might generalise it to other problems
   - They will implement the agreed solution several times and observe the effects
   - They will either decide that they don't require further help or that they do need such help and will contact the therapist or agency to access it. It is useful to say more about what this involves. I recommend informing the

28

client exactly what they need to do to access this help, what help is available and that they will be told how long they will need to wait for each mode of therapy delivery at that point to facilitate their decision.

Your client needs to know at the outset that they won't be able to make an appointment at the end of the conversation with you. The exception to this is if they are in a highly distressed state and/or at risk when the conversation ends. I usually make it clear that I regard the 'session' in SST as including the preparation work that the client does before we meet, the conversation itself and the time the client spends after the conversation, as specified in the Preface and in Point 2 see below.

In SST, a 'Session' includes:

- Preparation
- Conversation
- Implementation

It is also important for your client to know what your cancellation policy is as well as exceptions to absolute confidentiality.

When they have understood and agreed with all the above items, they can give their informed consent, and a contract is ready to be made. This contract can be verbal or written. I prefer to have a written contract with all my clients (in SST and longer-term work) as there is less chance of later misunderstanding when this is done.

When to Contract in SST

There is no definite time to make a contract with your SST clients. My own practice is for a person to sign and return my therapeutic contract before I send them my pre-conversation form, which is designed to help them prepare for the upcoming conversation (see Step 5). In some agencies, the contract is made at the beginning of the conversation as this is the first opportunity for this to be done. In other agencies, unless the client signs an online contract, they cannot access SST.

The important point is that the contract *is* made rather than *when* it is made.

Conversation Length

When I give workshops on SST, I am often asked how long a conversation is. While there is no definitive answer to this question, my response is as follows:

In my independent practice of SST, I tell clients that the conversation will last up to 50 minutes. The phrase 'up to' is important here since my client and I often complete the work before 50 minutes. When this happens, it is best to end the conversation at that point rather than use the remaining time discussing another of the client's problems when there is insufficient time to do this properly. Indeed, dealing with a second problem in these circumstances dilutes the work that we have done on their nominated problem. Thus, an SST conversation ends when the work is complete, not when the clock dictates the end.

Having said that, some agencies mandate their therapists to collect a lot of data on the client for various purposes, and this needs to be done before the therapeutic work can begin. In such cases, the conversation will be longer than 50 minutes, often lasting between 75-90 minutes.

Of course, whichever is the case, you need to inform your client about conversation length, and their agreement signifies that it is now part of your contract.

STEP 6

Invite Your Client to Nominate a Problem

This book focuses on using SST to help clients with their specific emotional and behavioural problems with which they have become stuck. One of the hallmarks of SST is getting down to business immediately, so it is important that you ask your client which problem they want to discuss with you.

The Importance of Language

The words you use in inviting your client to nominate a problem are important. Consider the following invitations:

- *What problem do you want to discuss with me today?*

This question allows your client to nominate whatever problem they choose. It is most consistent with the principle that SST is client-led.

- *What is your most pressing problem I can help you with today?*

This question limits your client to select their most pressing problem. However, they may not want to discuss their most pressing problem. Consequently, this question may not encourage them to discuss the problem they want to discuss.

- *If I could help you with one problem that would give you a sense that you were moving forward, which problem would that be?*

This question links addressing the client's nominated problem with 'moving forward'.

- *What problem are you stuck with that you would like to discuss with me so that I can help you get unstuck?*

This question focuses on stuckness and implies a goal of getting unstuck.

When a Client Has More than One Problem

Clients sometimes come to single-session therapy hoping to get help for more than one problem. Some SST therapists are clear that they will only work with one client problem in the session. They argue that if they promise to do more than that, they may both fail to deliver on their promise and fail to help the client with their nominated problem.

Other therapists are prepared to help their client with more than one problem, arguing that they will encourage the person to identify a linking theme and will work with that theme, thus working with more than one problem. I believe taking this latter tack is best done by experienced SST therapists. However, such therapists must judge whether a particular client will respond well to this thematic approach to SST.

I favour the one problem-at-a-time approach to working with problems in SST as it frees both therapist and client to focus on the client's nominated problem without the additional concern that they may not deal with the client's additional problem(s), As stated earlier, working with more than one problem in SST runs the risk of failing to help the client with either their nominated problem or their additional problem(s).

Given this, the purpose of inviting your client to select a nominated problem is to agree on the *one* problem the client wants to discuss with you.

STEP 7

Elicit a Conversation Goal from Your Client

Once you have encouraged your client to nominate a problem to discuss, it is important to know what your client wants to achieve by the end of their conversation with you. I call this the *conversation goal*.

One of your tasks as an SST therapist is to help your client be realistic about what to expect from SST. In my view, most of the time, you will not be able to help your client to render their problem a non-problem by the end of the conversation. What you can do is help your client develop a solution to the problem, which they can implement after the conversation.

Thus, for most clients who seek SST for help with a specific problem, assisting them in finding a solution to this problem constitutes a good conversation goal. Clients who say that by the end of the conversation, they would like some 'tools and techniques to help with my anxiety' (for example) are, in effect, telling you that they are looking for a solution to their problem in the form of 'tools and techniques'

Issues Concerning Conversation Goals

Your client may have one of several problematic conversation goals. Here is a partial list and how to respond to them.

'I want you to help me feel nothing'

Response: Feeling nothing is only possible when your client truly does not care about the issue. The fact is that your client does care about the issue. If they didn't, they would have the problem. Help your client to see that not caring about something that they care about is not possible. Show them instead that you can help them find a way of caring about the issue without disturbance rather than with the disturbance that they currently experience.

'I want you to help me feel less...... (e.g. anxious)'

Response: The difficulty with this conversation goal is that it assumes that less of a disturbed emotion is healthy. Encourage your client to see that you can help them respond to an adversity (in this case, *threat,* with a healthy emotion (e.g. non-anxious concern) rather than the diminution of an unhealthy emotion (e.g. anxiety).

'I don't know what my goal is'

Response: There are two ways of responding to this. The first is to ask the person to remember when they decided to seek help from you or the agency in which you work. Once they have done so, ask them what they hoped to get by the end of their first conversation with a therapist. The second way is to ask your client about their conversation goal options. You may have to start the ball rolling, but you can ask your client to join in once you have done so.

Understanding, Expression of Feelings and Searching for a Solution

When asked what they would like to achieve by the end of the conversation, your client might say that they would like to understand their problem better or express their feelings about it. In either case, you can ask them what they hope such understanding or expression of feelings would lead to. In such cases, your client is likely to say that they hope it will lead to them being able to solve their problem. In other words, understanding and feeling expression are deemed to have instrumental value for the client. This is fortuitous as these activities on their own are rarely sufficient for your client to solve their specific problem, although they may help in solution selection.

STEP 8

Agree on a Focus with Your Client, Stay Focused and Periodically Check that the Focus Is Still Relevant

A handful of clients come to single-session therapy wanting to use the opportunity to talk in an uninterrupted way about whatever concerns them. In this case, there is no need for you to create and agree on a focus with them. However, when your client is looking for a solution to a specific problem, you do need to co-create and agree on a focus with them and stay with it once it has been agreed.

Agreeing on a Focus

At this point of the process, you should have identified your client's nominated problem and their conversation goal. One or both of these components should provide you and your client with the focus of the conversation. Here is an example:

Therapist: To summarise. You are anxious about being rejected by women you are interested in and want to find a solution to this problem by the end of our conversation that you can implement afterwards. Is that right?

Client: Exactly.

Therapist: Shall we make this our focus for the conversation?

Client: That is what I would like.

Staying with the Agreed Focus

In my experience of training and supervising single-session therapists, they find it easier to agree on a focus than to stay with it. So, when the client moves away from the focus, the therapist tends to respond to what they said rather than bring the client back to the focus. The issue here is partly one of mindset. In therapy that is longer term, particularly at the beginning, the therapist will tend to follow the client rather than encourage them to develop a focus. However laudable this is in conventional therapy, it is not useful in SST where focused work is called for.

The Value of Interrupting the Client and How Best to Do So

When your client moves away from the focus, it is important that you interrupt them and bring them back to it. Before you do so, however, it is best for you to give your client a rationale for interrupting them, get their permission to do so, and, once this has been given, ask them how you can best do so. Here is an example:

Therapist: There may be times when I need to interrupt you to keep us both focused on what we have agreed to talk about. Does that make sense?

Client: Yes, it does. I know I can wander away from the topic.

Therapist: So, do I have your permission to interrupt you if necessary?

Client: Yes, indeed.

Therapist: From your perspective, how can I best interrupt you?

Client: Just say, 'I'd like to interrupt you'.

Periodically Checking that the Focus
Is Still Relevant

Although you have taken care to agree on a focus with your client based on their nominated problem and conversation goal, and you have helped them to stay with the focus, it is still a good idea to check with them periodically during the conversation that they are discussing what they have come to discuss. Very occasionally, a client realises that their nominated problem is not the issue they want to discuss and, if there is time, change tack and focus on the new issue.

STEP 9

Help Yourself and Your Client to Understand Their Nominated Problem and a Problem-Related Goal

I call myself an SST therapist who is concerned with my client's problem, solution and problem-related goal. However, there are SST therapists who are solution-focused in the sense that from the outset, they will help the client focus on finding a solution to their nominated problem, and in doing so, they will spend hardly any time on the client's problem. These therapists will bypass this step.

Once you and your client have agreed to focus on their nominated problem, it is important that you help both of you to understand (or assess) this problem.

Using Your Client's Data to Understand Their Problem

Initially, invite your client to tell you about their nominated problem as they see it. Learning about their problem from their perspective tells you about what they have included and excluded in their account, and this will provide you both with a shared platform to construct a fuller picture of your client's problem. Sometimes, the client's data is all the two of you need to co-create a solution to their problem. As you do this, it is important that you encourage them to share their perspective on the factors that contribute to their problem.

The Importance of Being Specific

Sometimes, your client's nominated problem will concern a specific *Situation*, in which case you can assess that *Situation*. At other times, your client's problem will be more general and you will need to ask them for a specific example of the problem. In these circumstances, you will find that working with specificity helps clarify the problem-related factors.

Understanding the Wider Context of the Problem

You may find it useful to understand the wider context in which the nominated problem occurs. Doing so sometimes provides factors that also contribute to the solution of the client's problem. For example, often, a female client will seek help for a relationship issue with one of their children. In addition to assessing the nature of this problem, you may wish to find out who else is involved in the issue and what their contribution may be to the problem. In this example, you may wish to enquire about the involvement of the client's partner and other children in the problem. Do they contribute to the problem, and can they contribute to the solution? Although you are doing individual SST, you can enrich that work by understanding the context or system in which the problem occurs.

Understanding Your Client's Nominated Problem through the Lens of Your Preferred Therapeutic Orientation(s)

It may well be that based on what your client has given you, you need to enrich your understanding of their nominated problem. To do this, you can draw insights from the therapeutic orientation(s) you favour. Different therapists will draw upon different therapeutic orientations. Let me share how I approach this task. Please note that this is only *one* way of doing so, not *the* way of doing so.

Using REBT's *Situational ABC* Framework

Rational Emotive Behaviour Therapy most informs my SST work, and I draw upon REBT's *Situational ABC* framework when necessary (see Table 1).

Table 1: REBT's *Situational ABC* Framework

Situation	
(A descriptive account of what happened when the problem occurred)	
Adversity (A)	
(What your client is most disturbed about in the *Situation*)	
Rigid/Extreme Basic Attitudes (B)	**Flexible/Non-Extreme Basic Attitudes (B)**
Consequences of AxB (C) • Emotional • Behavioural • Thinking	**Consequences of AxB (C)** • Emotional • Behavioural • Thinking

- I seek a clear description of the *Situation* in which the specific example of the client's nominated problem occurred.
- I look for what the client's main emotion was in that *Situation* and the behaviour and thinking that accompanied that emotion (*C*) (see Dryden, 2022).
- I use the client's *C* to find the adversity in the *Situation* (*A*) (i.e. what the client was most disturbed about in the *Situation*)
- I use *A* and *C* to discover the rigid/extreme attitude (at *B*) that the client held towards *A* that accounted for their problematic response at *C* and the flexible/non-extreme attitude alternative (also at *B*).

Problem-Maintaining Factors

I suggest you look more generally for how the client unwittingly maintains their problem. Examples of these problem-maintaining factors are avoidance, withdrawal, and the use of safety-seeking factors (both intrapersonal and interpersonal). The opposite of these factors can contribute to the client's solution.

Helping the Client to Formulate a Problem-Related Goal

Once you *identified* your client's nominated goal, then, as I have pointed out above, you need to identify what they want to achieve by the end of the conversation. This is their conversation goal (see Step 7. Once you have *assessed* your client's nominated problem, then you can help them set a goal related to this assessed problem. I call this their *problem-related goal*. The client must implement their selected solution after the conversation to achieve this goal. This is included in their implementation plan (see Step 16). The relationship between the client's nominated problem, conversation goal and problem-related goal is shown in Figure 1.

Nominated Problem → Conversation Goal → Problem-Related Goal Solution

Figure 1: The relationship between the client's nominated problem, conversation goal, and problem-related goal

Part 3

SST: The Middle Phase

Step 10

Enquire about Your Client's Past Attempts to Address Their Nominated Problem and Other Problems

Before you embark with your client searching for a solution to their nominated problem, it is useful to find out what past attempts your client has made to address this problem.

Enquiring about Successful Attempts to Solve the Nominated Problem

In general, people make quite a few attempts to deal with their problems before they seek professional help for them. Thus, they may seek help from their friends or relatives. They may go online to look for tools and techniques. Or they may have gone to therapy before to deal with the problem.

The fact that your client is seeking help for their nominated problem means that these attempts have not been fully successful. However, certain things they have tried might have yielded some benefits, and if so, you can use these helpful elements when you develop a solution with them.

Discovering what your client has done before to address their problem helps you to save time. Without doing so, you may spend time looking for a solution that your client may have already tried and which proved unsuccessful. Utilising time effectively and efficiently is a key SST value.

Enquiring about Successful Attempts to Solve Other Problems

If your client has found nothing helpful in their past attempts to address their nominated problem, you will have to look elsewhere for potentially useful strategies. There are two areas to investigate in this respect.

The first area is your client's experience dealing successfully with problems *related* to their nominated problem. If they have had such successful experiences in this area, discover what they did that was successful and see how they can transfer these strategies to their nominated problem. Ask them what would happen if they did this. Then, you can incorporate these strategies into the solution that you will both look for, which is designed to address their nominated problem effectively (see Step 14).

You can follow the same process in the second area: successful strategies that your client has employed to address other past problems that are *unrelated* to their nominated problem,

Attribute Any of Your Client's Successful Problem-Solving Strategies to their Ability as a Problem-Solver

By now, you have identified your client's successful experiences in dealing with their nominated problem and problems related and unrelated to their nominated problem. You have gathered useful information about the specific things that your client did to solve problems, particularly in the latter two areas. Not only can you explore with your client which of these strategies can be incorporated into the solution designed to help them deal effectively with their nominated problem, you can also help your client see themself as a person who can solve problems. This general therapeutic factor can be utilised later in the SST process.

Step 11

Forage for Internal and External Resources

I see myself as a forager when I do single-session therapy. What I mean by this is when I am working with a client, I am constantly searching for factors that my client can use in pursuit of their conversation and problem-related goals. These factors or resources relate to the person (internal resources) and the wider context in which your client lives (external resources).

Internal Resources

When your client seeks your help in SST, they come with one or more problems for which they need your assistance. One could say that they are in *problem mode*. However, it is vital that you keep in mind that it is certain that the person before you has a variety of resources that, while hidden from view, can contribute to the achievement of their goals. Paraphrasing from a phrase attributed to Aldous Huxley, 'There is nothing wrong with your client that what is right with them cannot fix.'[12]

It is useful to think of two categories of internal resources: tough-minded resources (including self-discipline, grit, persistence, and resilience) and tender-minded resources (including kindness, empathy, tenderness and compassion).

There are several ways of helping clients identify and acknowledge their internal resources: direct, indirect and inferred.

---

[12] 'There is nothing wrong with you that what's right with you cannot fix' – attributed to Aldous Huxley.

The Direct Way of Seeking Internal Resources

Perhaps the most obvious way of seeking your client's internal resources is to ask them directly. For example, 'What strengths do you have as a person that may help you address and solve the problem we are discussing?' If your client answers your question, all well and good. Note these strengths and use them later in the conversation to encourage your client to develop a solution (Step 14) and an implementation plan (Step 16). If they struggle to answer the question, it may be because they are preoccupied with their problem and find it difficult to focus on constructive aspects of themself or because they are modest and feel embarrassed about acknowledging their strengths.

A second direct way of seeking your client's internal resources is to ask them the following question, 'If you were being interviewed for a job that you really wanted and the interviewer asked you what your strengths were and you had to answer honestly, what would you say?' This question attempts to bypass the client's reticence and presents a scenario where sharing one's strengths may contribute to a valued outcome.

The Indirect Way of Seeking Internal Resources

A more indirect way of seeking the client's resources is to introduce another person into the field, such as a good friend. For example, 'If I asked a very good friend of yours who knows you very well what your strengths are, what would they say?' This question encourages your client to take a more objective approach to the question and to view themself through the eyes of someone well-disposed to them.

Inferring the Presence of Internal Resources from Your Client's Narrative

Another approach to discovering your client's strengths is to listen to their narrative and to infer the presence of such strengths from what they tell you. For example, 'Listening to your account of what you have been through, I am struck by your willingness to bear a lot for the sake of your children. Would you agree that this is one of your strengths?' If your client agrees then you can ask them what other strengths they have. Once a client has acknowledged that they have one strength, they may be more likely to identify others than if they haven't made such an acknowledgment.

External Resources

Another area of your client's life that provides possible resources that could be helpful to the work you are doing on the client's nominated problem is their external world. There are four potential sources here.

Other People

Other people in the client's life can be very useful in helping the client, particularly when it comes to the client implementing their solution. In this context, the concept of 'team', as in 'Who is on your team?' is valuable. The client is encouraged to think of people in their life as part of their 'team', with each person making a unique contribution to the client's life. This leads to the following question, 'Who on your team can provide help as you implement your chosen solution?' Your role here is to ensure that the assistance provided to the person is likely to be helpful.

Organisations

There may be organisations in the client's environment that can also be useful, depending on the nature of the client's nominated problem. For example, if your client is struggling with anxiety about public speaking, the work you will do with them can be supplemented by an organisation such as 'Toastmasters' where they can gain experience of speaking in front of an audience in a non-threatening environment designed to help people improve their communication skills in a public speaking context.

Other Helpful Resources

Other helpful resources such as self-help books, 'apps' and other materials can aid your client in achieving their problem-related goal. However, in suggesting such resources to your client, guard against overwhelming them with too many suggestions. In single-session therapy, it is important to realise that 'less is more'.

The Client's Immediate Environment

Finally, it is important to be aware of the client's immediate environment when talking to them, particularly online, as sometimes this environment can help you. For example, I was having a conversation with a client in SST and noticed that behind them was a poster with the following words:

> *Feelings are much like waves.*
> *We can't stop them from coming*
> *But we can choose which one to surf.*

The client's nominated problem concerned how they dealt with having many different thoughts in their mind. At a suitable point in the session, I asked my client to turn around and read the above words aloud. After they did so, I asked them to substitute the word 'feelings' with 'thoughts' and to speak aloud the modified verse. As they did so, they immediately saw the message's relevance for the solution to their problem and learning to 'surf my thoughts' became the dominant theme of our subsequent discussion.

Step 12

Elicit Your Client's Views on How to Solve Their Nominated Problem

Single-session therapy is client-led, and earlier, you would have encouraged your client to share their understanding of the factors that contributed to their problem (see Step 9). Similarly, it is important that you ask your client for their views of what constitutes a good solution to their problem.

It may be the case that your client does not have any ideas about how they can solve their problem, in which case you can proceed to help them develop a solution based on what the two of you have discussed so far and what your 'take' is on this issue (see Step 13).

On the other hand, your client may have views on how they can solve their problem, and if this is the case, your role is to take these views seriously and, in the first instance, evaluate the potential helpfulness of their suggestions.

While SST is client-led, this does not mean you have to stay silent if you have concerns about any of their suggestions.

For example:

Therapist: Do you have any ideas yourself about how you can solve your anxiety problem being criticised by your boss?

Client: Well, I was thinking about that. I know I have to see him some of the time, but I think the best thing I can do is to avoid him at all other times.

Therapist: Have you found that avoidance has been the best way of dealing with other anxiety issues that you may have or had in the past?

Client:	Put like that, I guess not.
Therapist:	Have you ever had the experience of being afraid of something and then, after facing what you feared, that fear began to diminish.
Client:	Yes, I used to be afraid of dogs, but I am not because I stopped avoiding them and began to face them.
Therapist:	So, what can you learn from that experience that may be relevant to dealing with your anxiety problem with your boss?
Client:	It is best to face my boss rather than take every opportunity to avoid him. But facing him on its own isn't going to work. I need something to deal with anxiety.
Therapist:	Would you be interested in finding a solution which involves you facing your boss as often as you can, but dealing with his criticism in a healthier way?
Client:	Yes.

In the above exchange, the client offers a solution that, in the therapist's opinion, won't work. Rather than telling the client that, the therapist, using Socratic questioning, helps the client to see that.

The following is a sample of client-suggested solutions that, in all probability, won't work. It is your job, as a therapist, to deal with these occurrences in a similar way to the therapist in the above exchange by helping your clients to see that the suggested solutions won't work in the long run and keeping the door open for an exploration of alternative more constructive solutions.

- Avoidance of the problem-related adversity
- The use of intrapersonal safety-seeking strategies that interfere with the client facing the adversity
- The use of interpersonal safety-seeking strategies (e.g. relying on others but not in a way that supports the client's problem-solving resources

- Seeking reassurance from others when the client is not re-assurable
- Using solutions that have not worked but continuing to use them in the belief that they will work eventually if the client persists for long enough

Step 13

Offer Your 'Take' to Your Client

In single-session therapy, the therapist is cautioned against being 'an expert' where definitive statements about the nature of the client's problem and how to address it effectively are made. However, in my view, this does not mean that therapist cannot share their expertise when necessary if the client is prepared to hear it.

When helping your client to develop a solution, you may find that there is not enough 'on the table' to help your client construct one. This is one case where you can offer your client your 'take' on what they can do to address their problem effectively by constructing and implementing such a solution. The important issue here is that you need to offer your client your 'take' and not give it until the client has agreed that you can do so. Before doing so, it is important that you do two things. First, you need to clarify that your 'take' represents *one* perspective on a solution and not *the* perspective. Stress that there are other perspectives. Second, emphasise that if the client does not resonate with your 'take', it is important that they feel free to tell you. Indeed, inform them that sometimes, when a client finds a therapist's suggested solution not useful when they explain why, their explanation can shed light on what might constitute a constructive solution.

One Therapist's 'Take'

In Step 9, I outlined REBT's *Situational ABC* framework when outlining my 'take' on understanding the client's nominated problem if I need to introduce it. If I have done so, the client will be able to see that one solution to their problem involves changing their rigid/extreme attitude to its flexible/non-

58

extreme attitude. Indeed, even if I have not previously introduced the *Situational ABC* framework, I would offer this attitudinal-based solution to a client to see how useful it might be to them.

While many of the practical ideas in this book come from the single-session therapy mindset (see Step 2), when you offer your client your take on their nominated problem and how it may be addressed, you are drawing from your favoured therapeutic orientation(s). It is at this point that the diversity of single-session therapy work is most apparent.

Step 14

Help Your Client to Construct a Solution

In this step, I will consider the factors you can draw on while helping your client construct a solution to their nominated problem. I will also briefly consider the different types of solutions that you and your client can consider.

On Helping Your Client to Develop a Solution

Table 2 (next page) outlines the factors you and your client can draw upon while working together to find a solution to their nominated problem, several of which I have already discussed. These factors should be considered as a handy person considers tools in a toolbox – important to have at your disposal, but you will not use all of the tools while fixing every problem. It is also important to note that some of the factors listed in Table 2 that you and your client are likely to use will emerge from the conversation that you have been having. Conversely, it will become clear which factors you will not be drawing upon again from your conversation.

It may be that one solution stands out for you both, and your client feels able to commit to the solution going forward. In which case you can move to Step 15. On the other hand, if two or three possible solutions seem to have potential, it is useful to engage your client in a brief cost-benefit analysis of these solutions to determine the one to which the client is prepared to commit.

Table 2   Factors to draw upon when helping your client construct a solution to their nominated problem

---

- Internal Strengths
- External Resources
- Role Models
- Guiding Principles (e.g. 'Do, Don't Stew')
- Your Client's Prior Helpful and Unhelpful Attempts to Solve the Problem
- Exceptions: When the Problem Does Not Occur
- Instances of the Client's Goal Occurring
- Experiences of Solving the Problem in a Different Area
- Successful Experiences of Solving Problems Unrelated to the Nominated Problem
- The Opposite of the Client's Problem-Maintenance Factors
- How the Client Views the Solution to the Client's Nominated Problem
- How the Therapist Views the Solution to the Client's Nominated Problem

---

Different Types of Solutions

There are different types of solutions that you and your client can consider. I will briefly review them here.

A Reframing Solution

When employing a reframing solution, you help your client to put their problem or problematic event into a new frame with the result that the problem is rendered non-problematic and can even be seen in a positive light (e.g. seeing hurt feelings as evidence that your client cares).

An Attitude Change Solution

An attitude is an evaluative stance that your client takes towards an adversity. Here, the client's nominated problem is likely to be determined by them holding a rigid/extreme attitude towards the adversity. Helping them to develop a flexible/non-extreme attitude here will help them solve their problem, particularly when backed up with appropriate action.

An Inference Change Solution

An inference is your client's hunch about the *Situation* that leads them to infer the presence of an adversity. This inference may be correct or incorrect. Helping your client to make a more realistic inference about the *Situation* can often be helpful.

A Solution Based on a Change in the Person's Relationship with the Problem

Sometimes, you can help your client by encouraging them to shift their relationship to their problem. This may involve them recognising what they saw as a dysfunctional response to an adversity was, in fact, quite an understandable one which many people would have made. This helps the person accept their response's existence rather than fight against it. Indeed, some therapists would argue that your client's struggle with their problematic emotions and thoughts is the problem. It follows that if you help your client stop struggling against these responses and accept their existence instead, this may constitute a good solution to their problem (Bennett & Oliver, 2019).

A Behavioural Change Solution

When your client adopts a solution based on behaviour change their change in behaviour invites a different response from another person with whom they have a problem. Behaviour change does not guarantee that the other person will respond constructively, but it will increase the chances of this occurring.

A *Situational* Change Solution

Sometimes, your client can best help themself if they change a problematic *Situation* that they are in. For example, your client may be sharing a flat with two people who dislike them, making their life difficult. If no other solution will help your client, moving accommodation is probably in their best interest.

A Combination of Solutions

While a single solution to your client's nominated problem may suffice (e.g. reframing), more often they need a combination of solutions. For example, if your client needs to establish boundaries with their mother, they need to change not only their behaviour but also their attitude in a way that supports boundary setting.

Step 15

Invite Your Client to Rehearse Their Constructed Solution

Once you and your client have agreed on a solution to their nominated problem, it is important that you invite them to rehearse it before you go on to develop an implementation plan (see Step 16). Imagine that you are in the market for a new car. Would you buy a car without taking it out for a test drive? Of course, you wouldn't. It may be a good car, but you need to find out if it suits you in terms of ease of handling the controls and comfort, for example. The only way you can discover that is by driving the car. The same is true for the solution that you and your client have co-created.

Determination of Solution Viability

Thus, before your client commits to carrying out the solution, they need to satisfy themself that they can see themself implementing it and that there are no unforeseen difficulties with the solution, for example. Thus, the first reason to invite your client to rehearse the solution is to help them judge its viability. This is why I call this *determination of solution viability*. If the solution is viable, then some 'tweaks' may need to be made to it before the client fully commits themself to it. If it is not viable, the next most promising solution can be chosen and rehearsed.

Preparation for Solution Implementation

The main reason for using rehearsal of the solution at *this* stage of the process is to help the client determine solution viability, there is another reason to employ it. Once the client has deemed the solution viable, the second reason to use it is to give them practice of the solution before they implement it in their life. This is why I call this *preparation for solution implementation*. Doing this can reveal unforeseen obstacles which can be dealt with in advance.

Methods of Solution Rehearsal

As noted above, solution rehearsal can be used in SST to help the client determine the viability of a solution and to give them practice with it before real-world implementation. Here is a sample of such methods.

Chairwork

Chairwork involves the client addressing their problem while using chairs to facilitate dialogue between self and others or between different parts of self. As such, chairwork allows the client to rehearse their chosen solution where it involves such dialogue.

Role-play

Sometimes a client is uncomfortable using chairwork and may prefer to rehearse their selected solution in a role-play scenario with you, as therapist, playing the role of the other person or that part of themself that the client needs to have a conversation with. When you play a role in the role-play, your client must brief you well so you can play the role accurately.

Imagery

When using imagery (or mental rehearsal) to rehearse a solution, the client must see themself enacting the solution in a coping capacity rather than masterfully. In the former case, they see themself initially implementing the solution with difficulty but persisting until they do it well. In the latter case, they see themself implementing the solution without any struggle. The former is realistic, while the latter is not.

Step 16

Develop an Implementation Plan with Your Client and Identify and Deal with Obstacles to Implementation

At this point, your client has committed themself to the solution and is ready to make a plan about how to implement it in their life. It is important that you remember that in more conventional therapy, you would negotiate a specific homework assignment, which you would review in the following session. By contrast, in single-session therapy, since you may not see your client again, you need to equip them with a general plan to help them implement the solution in relevant circumstances in their life.

Components of an Implementation Plan

The following are the components of a good implementation plan:

- The solution to be implemented
- The purpose of implementing the solution
- Where the solution is to be implemented
- When the solution is to be implemented.
- How often is the solution to be implemented.
- If the solution is to be implemented with other people, these people should be specified in the plan.

It is important to recognise that the more your client can integrate the action plan into their everyday life, the more likely it is that they will be able to implement it.

Identifying and Dealing with Potential Obstacles

After you have developed an implementation plan with your client and the guidelines for putting this plan into practice have been agreed upon, it is important for you to explore with your client what obstacles they may encounter in carrying out the plan.

Once you have identified such obstacles, begin by focusing on the one your client thinks they need to tackle first, which, if overcome, would give them the best chance of implementing the plan. Once you have done this, suggest to your client an imagery exercise, where your client encounters the obstacle mentioned above and sees themself dealing with it constructively before picturing themself implementing the action plan.

You probably don't have time to do this with every obstacle your client identifies, so you can suggest they use this process with any other obstacles later, if necessary.

Part 4

SST: The Ending Phase and Beyond

Step 17

Invite Your Client to Summarise the Conversation

How do you know when you are entering the ending phase with your client? In my view, while there are no definitive markers that indicate that your conversation with your client is coming to an end, one reliable sign that the end of the conversation is approaching is when you have helped your client construct an implementation plan and helped them identify and deal with any obstacles to carrying out this plan in their everyday life.

At this point, you can inform your client that your work is ending and invite them to summarise the conversation. Your client may be surprised you asked them to do this because they may think this is your task. Indeed, you may think it is more appropriate to summarise the conversation for the client. However, this would not be in keeping with the single-conversation mindset, which stresses the primacy of your client's perspective[13]. Additionally, your client remains active when they summarise the conversation, while they become passive when you do this for them. So, you may need to provide your client with a rationale for them to summarise the conversation as in the following:

Therapist: We are approaching the end of our time together, so could you summarise what we have covered in our conversation today?

---

[13] Some agencies mandate their therapists to provide clients with a written summary of the conversation, which is then emailed to them. If you work for such an agency, then you must do this. However, there is nothing to stop you from asking the client for their summary and emailing this to them after the conversation, reminding them that this was their summary, not yours.

Client: You want *me* to summarise. I'm not good at things like that. Can't you summarise what we have talked about?

Therapist: I could summarise the conversation, but I have found that when clients do this, they do so from their perspective and emphasise points that they think have been important for them. When I provide a summary, I am necessarily doing so from my perspective. As such, I am speculating what you have found important, and I may be wrong about this. Also, you are more likely to take away points vital to you when you summarise the conversation than points that I think are important to you when I summarise.

Client: OK. That makes sense. I'll give it a go.

In my experience, clients are generally good at summarising the conversation, much better than they think they will be. Ideally, the client's summary should include their nominated problem, solution, and implementation plan. If, in your opinion, they have omitted something important concerning these areas, then you could mention it and see if they agree with you.

Step 18

Elicit Your Client's Takeaways

A therapy 'takeaway' is a point deemed important enough by your client that they will remember it after the conversation and be guided by it. It will also influence their future behaviour concerning their nominated problem and perhaps other areas too (see Step 19).

Your client's takeaways should include their selected solution, and if it doesn't, this needs to be explored with them. Asking your client for their takeaways is important because, in addition to their selected solution, they may mention other points, too.

While your client's summary is likely to provide an overview of what you covered in the conversation with them, their takeaways refer to points that they have learned from the conversation that could make a difference in their life in the future.

It may be that the client's summary and their takeaways are the same. In which case, don't worry about that. However, they may be different, and that is why I suggest that you ask about both.

In my independent SST practice, I send my clients an audio recording of the conversation and a transcript of the conversation for their later review.[14]. I have found that what some clients take away from the conversation only becomes apparent once they have listened to the recording and/or read the transcript.

---

[14] I am not suggesting that you do this routinely with your SST clients. It is just my practice. The audio recording of the conversation is included in the price of the session. If they want a transcript of the session. I pass on to them what it costs me to have the conversation transcribed by the professional transcriber that I use.

Step 19

Encourage Your Client to Generalise Their Learning

Your client may have sought SST because they have been struggling with one problem for which they are seeking a solution. Your primary task in the conversation is to help them to achieve what they have come for. However, they may have other problems they have chosen not to discuss with you. In both scenarios, if feasible, it is a good idea to ask your client how they might generalise their learning to other problems they may have. You need to take care when you do this. Otherwise, the client may take this as a cue to discuss one of their other problems. If this happens, you need to interrupt your client and explain that your purpose is to help them see the possibilities of what they have learned from the conversation rather than work on their other problems with you.

In Step 4, I discussed the issue of the length of a therapy conversation in SST. Once you have concluded your work on the client's nominated problem and you still have time remaining, then it is far better to spend this time encouraging your client to think about how they may implement their learning in other areas in their life than it is to begin to work on a new problem. Generally, you will not have time to do this, and if you try to do so, it will interfere with your client's learning from the work you did with them on their nominated problem.

Finally, when discussing the issue of generalising learning with your client, it is useful to suggest to them that they make a written list of areas where they can do this for later review.

Step 20

Discuss How Your Client May Access Further Help

In the Preface and in Step 4, I made the point that a 'session' in SST includes (i) the preparation work that your client does before they meet with you, (ii) the conversation that they have with you in person or online to discuss their nominated problem and (iii) the time they spend after the conversation reflecting on what they have learned from the conversation, digesting their learning, implementing the solution to their nominated problem and, if relevant, to other areas and seeing the outcome of all this work before deciding whether or not they need additional help. Thus, unless they are in crisis or highly distressed at the end of their conversation with you, do not make another appointment with them because, as defined above, the 'session' has not finished.

When the 'session' by this definition has finished, and your client decides that they do not need further help, the SST process will have ended. However, if they do need further help, you should remind them of what you told them during contracting about accessing this help (see Step 4). This should include:

- *Who they should contact to access further help and how they can make contact.*

- *The help that is available to them.* In my case, the modes of therapy that I offer are listed and described on my website. Thus, they may choose to have another conversation with me, a contracted number of conventional therapy sessions or ongoing therapy. Ideally, in therapy agencies, clients should also be able to select the mode of therapy delivery that they think best suits their needs, but there may be restrictions to them doing so. What is important is that clients are clear about what is available to them.

- *The time they will have to wait to access their chosen mode of therapy delivery.* You will not know this at the end of your conversation because you do not know when the client will return if they choose to do so. However, remind them that they will be informed of waiting times at the time of their request for further help.

- *Inform them about what can be done if they request help that you or your agency do not provide.* In this case, be clear about what you can and can't do. Thus, you might tell them that if they want help that you or your agency do not provide, you may be able to refer them to a different therapist or agency providing that help, but if you can't, they will have to make their own enquiries.

Step 21

Deal with any Unfinished Business with Your Client

Many years ago, Jerome Frank (1961) made the point that while people seek therapy for various troublesome symptoms and complex problems, they are often demoralised. Your task in SST, then, is not only to help your client with their specific nominated problem but also to help restore their morale. This is primarily done by helping your client see that they *can* deal with their nominated problem by implementing the solution you have co-created and by helping them with a plan to put it into practice. It is also done by ending the conversation well.

The latter is done by asking your client two questions and responding to their answers.

- 'Do you have anything to tell me about what we have been discussing today that you would regret not telling me once you think about our conversation later?'
- 'Do you have anything to ask me about what we have been discussing today that you would regret not asking me once you think about our conversation later?'

It would be best if you strived, therefore, to help your client leave the conversation focused on their implementation plan and other takeaways rather than on any regrets they may have about not sharing critical information with you and not asking you key questions. Put differently, you don't want your client to have any unfinished business once they think about the conversation later.

In asking these questions, make sure that the focus is on the nominated problem that you have been discussing with them. If the client uses your question to begin to tell you about a second problem, tactfully interrupt them (see Step 8) and return to their nominated problem, having explained why.

Step 22

Seek Immediate Feedback from Your Client

In conventional therapy, the purpose of seeking your client's feedback at the end of a conversation is twofold. First, it helps you deal with issues that might otherwise preoccupy the client negatively after the session. This is relevant for SST, and as such, you can ask your client such questions as

- How do you feel about how our conversation went?
- Did you struggle with anything in our conversation today?
- Is there something important we missed today?
- Did anything come up in our conversation that you didn't expect?

If your client mentions something that needs to be dealt with before they leave, then it is
important that you do so.

Second, your client's end-of-conversation feedback helps you calibrate your future behaviour to meet your client's needs better. Since you may not see your client again in SST, this is less relevant than the first purpose.

There is a third reason for seeking feedback from your clients. This is to help you better calibrate your SST work with future clients. The best way to do this is to ask all your clients if they would be prepared to complete a brief form so that you know how helpful the conversation was for them. Once they agree, send them a form to complete and return (see Appendix 3).

Ideally, your client should send it back to someone other than you since it is challenging to be critical if your client knows you will read the form.

Such a form can be useful for an agency offering SST as it will help them monitor clients' experiences who see different therapists. This will help them to identify therapists who are not seen as helpful and thus prompt remedial action on behalf of the agency.

Step 23

Seek Longer-Term Feedback from Your Client

In addition to getting immediate feedback from your client, in my view, it is important to get longer-term feedback from them. I say 'in my view' here because some single-session therapists believe that in SST, the client should only have one contact with the therapist and no more. From this perspective, you would not seek longer-term evaluative feedback from your client since this would be another contact.[15]

However, most SST therapists believe that this mode of therapy delivery does not preclude further help from being available to clients. They hold that SST can be enhanced by both pre-conversation contact and longer-term feedback. So, what are the reasons to seek longer-term feedback from your client?

Why Seek Longer-Term Feedback from Your Client?

Seeking longer-term feedback has the following purposes:

- It allows your client to report on what they have done since their conversation with you. In my experience, many clients appreciate such an opportunity.
- It provides outcome evaluation data (i.e. how the client has done). Such information can help you improve your delivery of SST. It also allows you to demonstrate to

---

[15] These therapists would also not ask clients to complete a pre-conversation form before seeing them since this would constitute another contact.

others the longer-term effects of this mode of therapy when they enquire.

- It provides the agency where you work offering SST with service evaluation data (the client's experience of seeking help from the agency). Such data can help the organisation improve its SST service.

When to Seek Longer-Term Feedback from Your Client?

When longer-term feedback is scheduled depends on whether SST therapy takes place in a therapist's independent practice or an agency. If you work in independent practice, you and your client decide when to schedule this contact. However, if you work in an agency, that decision will have been made by the agency's management.

My Approach to Seeking Longer-Term Feedback from Clients

Here, I will discuss seeking longer-term feedback from a client who has decided they got what they wanted from their first and only SST conversation with me.[16]

I used to seek longer-term feedback from my clients by telephone. While this was interactive and enabled me to follow up on some of a person's responses, it made the SST package more expensive as I would build in the cost of this mode of seeking feedback in the price of the overall package. For this reason, I now use a questionnaire to seek longer-term feedback from a client, which I do between two and three months after the session, depending on the client's view. I have presented my

---

[16] When an SST client accesses more help in SST, I would still recommend seeking longer-term feedback from them on their experience of the conversation that they had with you. Do this in the same way as you would do it if they decided not to access further help.

longer-term feedback questionnaire in Appendix 4. Please note that I choose not to use objective forms to measure outcomes. I do realise, however, that many single-session therapists employ such measures, and if you do, you will need to give these to the client to complete pre-conversation and when you contact them for longer-term feedback.

Postscript

We have now reached the end of this step-by-step guide to practising SST when your client has a specific problem. I hope you have found it useful and would appreciate any feedback you have for me that might improve this book's future editions. Please email me at windy@windydryden.com

Appendix 1

What is Single-Session Therapy (SST): Information for Prospective Clients
Windy Dryden PhD

- Single-Session Therapy is an intentional endeavour where you and I set out with the purpose of helping you in one conversation, on the understanding that more help is available

- In SST, therapy takes place one contact at a time, and one contact may be all the time that you need. At the end of the conversation, I will invite you to reflect on and digest what you learned from it, act on what you learned and see what happens before you decide whether to seek further help. In SST, a block of conversations is not offered routinely to you but can be done so, if you and I decide that this is indicated

- SST is based on the principle of offering help at the point of need rather than at the point of availability. It has the effect of you being seen quickly, when you need help

- SST is based on three foundations:
  - The most frequent number of conversations clients have internationally is '1', followed by '2', '3', and so on
  - 70–80% of those who have one conversation are satisfied with it given their current circumstances
  - Therapists are poor at predicting who will attend for only one conversation and who will attend for more

- My goals in SST are:
  - To help you get 'unstuck'
  - To help you take a few steps forward, which may encourage you to travel the rest of the journey without my professional assistance
  - To help you address a specific issue

- I will encourage you to prepare for our conversation so that you get the most from it, and to this end, I will send you a pre-conversation form for you to complete.

- The focus of a conversation in SST is on us negotiating a goal for the conversation, after which I will help you to find and rehearse a solution that facilitates the achievement of this goal. Then, I will help you to devise an action plan which you can implement after the conversation.

- In SST, I will help you to:
  - Discover what you have done in the past to deal with your problem. I will then encourage you to use what has been helpful and set aside what has not been helpful
  - Identify and use your internal strengths and external resources in implementing the agreed solution

- I encourage follow-up to discover how you are getting on and to improve service delivery.

Appendix 2

Pre-Conversation Form[17]

I invite you to fill in this form before we meet. This will help you to prepare for the conversation so that you can get the most from it. It also helps me to help you as effectively as I can. Please return it by email attachment before our conversation. Be brief and concise in your answers.

1. **What is the issue that you want to focus on with me?**
   Be concise. In one or two sentences get to the heart of the problem, if possible.

2. **Why is this significant?**
   What's at stake? How does this affect your life? What is the future impact if the issue is not resolved?

3. **What is your goal in discussing this issue?**
   What are the specific results you would like to achieve by the end of the conversation that would give you the sense that you have begun to make progress on the issue?

4. **Why now?**
   Why are you seeking help for this issue at this time?

5. **How have you tried to deal with the issue up to this point?**
   What steps, successful or unsuccessful have you taken so far in addressing the issue?

6. **What are the strengths or inner resources that you have as a person that you could draw upon while tackling the issue?**

---

[17] Please note that on the actual form, there are boxes in which the client can write their responses.

If you struggle with answering this question, think of what people who really know you and who are on your side would say.

7. **Who are the people in your life who can support you as you tackle the issue?**
Name them and say what help each can provide.

8. **What help do you hope I can best provide you? Please check the main <u>one</u>. Do not check more than one box.**

- ☐ Help me to develop greater understanding of the issue
- ☐ Help me by just listening while I talk about the issue
- ☐ Help me to feel heard and understood
- ☐ Help me to express my feelings about the issue
- ☐ Help me to solve an emotional or behavioural problem; help me get unstuck
- ☐ Help me to make a decision
- ☐ Help me to resolve a dilemma
- ☐ Help me by signposting me to the most appropriate service for my situation
- ☐ Other (please specify):

Appendix 3

Single-Session Therapy Conversation Rating Scale [SST-CRS]

Name: Date:

It is very important for me to monitor my counselling work. So, please rate the conversation you recently had with me by <u>underlining</u> the number that best fits your experience on the following scales.

The pre-conversation questionnaire was not useful in helping me to prepare for the conversation   **0 1 2 3 4 5 6 7 8 9 10**   The pre-conversation questionnaire was useful in helping me to prepare for the conversation

I did not feel heard, understood or respected by Windy Dryden during our conversation   **0 1 2 3 4 5 6 7 8 9 10**   I did feel heard, understood and respected by Windy Dryden during our conversation

Windy Dryden and I did not discuss what I I wanted to discuss   **0 1 2 3 4 5 6 7 8 9 10**   Windy Dryden and I did discuss what I wanted to discuss

Windy Dryden's approach was not a good fit for me   **0 1 2 3 4 5 6 7 8 9 10**   Windy Dryden's approach was a good fit for me

Overall, I did not get what I wanted from my conversation with Windy Dryden   **0 1 2 3 4 5 6 7 8 9 10**   Overall, I did get what I wanted from my conversation with with Windy Dryden

If I wanted more help, I would not choose Windy Dryden as my counsellor   **0 1 2 3 4 5 6 7 8 9 10**   If I wanted more help, I would choose Windy Dryden as my counsellor

Finally, if there was anything that was particularly useful or anything I could have done to have improved the conversation we had, please let me know in the box below:

```
┌──────────────────────────────────────────────┐
│                                              │
│                                              │
│                                              │
│                                              │
└──────────────────────────────────────────────┘
```

Thank you for your feedback. Please email this form back to _____

Appendix 4

Single-Session Therapy
Longer-Term Feedback Questionnaire

Name: Date:

Please type your responses in the spaces provided.

Question	**Response**
1. What progress did you make on the issue that you brought to our conversation. Indicate the amount of progress you have made on this issue by using a 0% (no progress) - 100% (problem solved) scale.	Issue Brought to the Conversation (Please name this): Amount of progress made: Factors that helped me make progress: Factors that were absent that could have helped me make more progress:
2. Did you make any progress on other issues that you have that you did not bring to our conversation? Please elaborate.	

3. How would you describe your relationship with Windy Dryden during the conversation?	
4. What, if anything, did Windy Dryden do during the conversation that was helpful to you?	
5. What, if anything, did Windy Dryden do during the conversation that was unhelpful to you?	
6. How helpful did you find the pre-conversation form if you were sent one? Please elaborate.	
7. How helpful did you find the audio-recording of your conversation with Windy Dryden? Please elaborate.	
8. How helpful did you find the transcript of your conversation with Windy Dryden? Please elaborate.	
9. How does Single-Session Therapy compare with other therapies that you have had? Please elaborate.	

10. What improvements, if any, do you think need to be made to the Single-Session Therapy framework?	
11. Please give any additional feedback that your responses to the questions above have not covered.	

Thank you very much for your cooperation.

Please send your completed form back to me at: _____

Windy Dryden

References

Bennett, R., & Oliver, J.E. (2019). *Acceptance and Commitment Therapy: 100 Key Points and Techniques.* Routledge.

Cannistrà, F. (2022). The single conversation therapy mindset: Fourteen principles gained through an analysis of the literature. *International Journal of Brief Therapy and Family Science, 12*(1), 1–26.

Cooper, M., & Law, D. (2018). (Eds.), *Working with Goals in Counselling and Psychotherapy.* Oxford University Press.

Dryden, W. (2023). *ONEplus Therapy: Help at the Point of Need.* Onlinevents Publications.

Dryden, W. (2024). *Single-Session Therapy: 100 Key Points and Techniques. 2nd edition.* Routledge.

Dryden, W. (2025). Bringing a single-conversation mindset to counselling in an online health service in the UK. In Hoyt, M.F., & Cannistra, F. (eds). *Single Session Therapies: Why and How One-At-A-Time Mindsets Are Effective.* Routledge.

Frank, J.D. (1961). *Persuasion and Healing: A Comprehensive Study of Psychotherapy.* The Johns Hopkins Press.

Hoyt, M.F., Young, J., & Rycroft, P. (2021). (Eds.). *Single Conversation Thinking and Practice in Global, Cultural and Familial Contexts: Expanding Applications.* Routledge.

Norcross, J.C., & Cooper, M. (2021). *Personalizing Psychotherapy: Assessing and Accommodating Patient Preferences.* American Psychological Association.

Simon, G.E., Imel, Z.E., Ludman, E.J., & Steinfeld, B.J. (2012). Is dropout after a first psychotherapy visit always a bad outcome? *Psychiatric Services, 63*(7), 705-707.

Index

A 43, 44
adversity 36, 43, 44, 56, 62
anxiety 35, 36, 38, 53, 55, 56
assessment 11, 18
assess problems, not people 18
attitude change solution 62
avoidance 44, 55, 56

B 43, 44
beginning phase 8, 25–45
behavioural change solution 62–3
behavioural consequences 43
behavioural problem 7, 32, 33, 87
Bennett, R. 62, 93
build on what client has done before 22

C 43, 44
cancellation policy 29
Cannistrà, F. 10n, 93
chairwork 65
client choice 19
client–therapist relationship 13
complex problem may not require
    complex solution 23–4
consequences 18, 43
contract with your client 28–30
    what constitutes 28–9
    when to, in SST 29–30
conversation 7
    invite client to prepare for 31–2
    invite client to summarise 71–2
    length 30
    tailored to client 12
conversation goal 35
    elicit from your client 35–7
    issues concerning 35–6
Cooper, M. 10n, 93

disseminate your service to potential
    clients and stakeholders 19
disturbance 36
Dryden, Windy 7, 8, 10, 13, 44, 83, 84,
    88, 91–3

emotional consequences 43
emotional problem 7
ending phase and beyond 8, 69–83
end-of-conversation goal, negotiating with
    client 21
equip client with solution for later
    application 23
exceptions: when problem does not occur
    61
experience 8, 36, 50, 53, 56, 61, 72, 80–2,
    88
expression of feelings 36–7
external resources
    client's immediate environment 54
    organisations 53
    other helpful resources 54
    other people 53

feedback from client
    seek immediate 79–80
    seek longer-term 81–3
    WD's approach to seeking longer-term
        82–3
    when to seek longer-term 82
    why seek longer-term 81–2
feeling less 36
feeling nothing 36
feelings 36, 37, 54, 61, 87
flexible/non-extreme basic attitudes 43,
    44, 58, 62
focus
    agree on with client 38–40
    periodically checking still relevant 40
    staying with agreed 39
    on what is right with client, not what is
        wrong 12
form completion 31
Frank, Jerome 77, 93
further help, discuss how client my access
    75–6

generalise learning 74
goals 9, 10, 13, 21, 22, 34–8, 40, 41, 44,
    45, 51, 54, 61, 84–6

goals (continued)
  'I don't know what my goal is' 36
  instances of occurring 61
  guiding principles 61

help at point of need 17–14
helping client to understand problem 22
Hoyt, M.F. 10n, 93
Huxley, Aldous 51

imagery 66
Imel, Z.E. 12, 93
implementation plan 67
  components 67
  develop with client and identify and
    deal with obstacles to 67–8
  identifying and dealing with potential
    obstacles 68
inference change solution 62
informed consent 11n, 28, 29
initial step in right direction, helping client
    take 23
internal resources 51–3
  direct way of seeking 52
  indirect way of seeking 52
  inferring presence of from client's
    narratives 52–3
interrupting client 39
interpersonal safety-seeking strategies 56
intrapersonal safety-seeking strategies 56

language
  importance of 33–4
Law, D. 10n, 93
Ludman, E.J. 12, 93

middle phase 8, 47–68

nominated problem 18n
  agree on 21
  elicit client's views on how to solve
    55–7
  enquire about client's past attempts to
    address 49–50
  enquire about successful attempts to
    solve 49
  help yourself and client to understand
    41–5

nominated problem (continued)
  invite client to nominate problem 33–4
  speaking it helps find solution 22
  understanding wider context of 42
  using client's data to understand 41
  when client has more than one 34
Norcross, J.C. 10n, 93

offer your 'take' to client 58–9
Oliver, J.E. 62, 93
open-access, enter now 7
organisations 53–4
other problems
  enquire about client's past attempts to
    address 49–50
  enquire about successful attempts to
    solve 49

permission to interrupt client 39
pre-conversation phase 8, 15–24
pre-conversation preparation form 31–2,
    86–7
problem-focused 21
problem-maintaining factors 44
  opposite of 61
problem-related goal 44–5
problem-solving 12
problem-solving strategies 50

Rational Emotive Behaviour Therapy
    (REBT) 43, 58
  Situational ABC framework 43–4, 58–9
reassurance 57
REBT *see* Rational Emotive Behaviour
    Therapy
reflect-digest-act-decide process 11
reframe problem, helping client to 23
reframing solution 61
respond to first contact 27
rigid/extreme basic attitudes 43
role models 61
role-play 65
Rycroft, P. 10n, 93

set up practice and disseminate 17–19
Steinfeld, B.J. 13, 93
session, definition of in SST 7
Simon, G.E. 13, 93

single-session therapy (SST) 7
  client-led 12
  client suitability for 18
  Conversation Rating Scale [SST-CRS]
    88–9
  information for prospective clients 84–5
  longer-term feedback questionnaire 90–2
  nature of 9–10
  therapist 8
  transparent 12
  what is it? 9–13, 84–5
single-session therapy mindset 10–13
  adopt to help client with specific
    problem 20–4
Situation 42
Situational change solution 63
Socratic questioning 56
solution-focused help 7
solutions to nominated problem
  attitude change 62
  based on change in person's
    relationship with problem 62
  behavioural change solution 62–3
  combination of 63
  determination of viability 64
  different types of 61–3
  help client construct 60–3
  help client develop 60–1
  how client views 61
  how therapist views 61
  inference change 62
  invite client to rehearse their
    constructed 64–6
  methods of rehearsal 65–6
  preparation for implementation 65
  reframing 61
  searching for 36–7
  Situational change 63

solving problem
  client's prior attempts at 61
  experiences of, in a different area 61
  successful experiences of, unrelated to
    nominated problem 61
specific, importance of being 42
SST *see* single-session therapy
Steinfeld, B.J. 93
summarise conversation, invite client to
  71–2
supervision 8
synchronous communication 9

takeaways, client 73
therapeutic focus, co-creating 22
therapeutic orientation(s) 42–3
thinking consequences 43
thoughts 54
tools and techniques 35
training 8

understanding 36–7
  nominated problem through lens of
    your preferred therapeutic
    orientation(s) 42–3
  wider context of problem 42
unfinished business with client, deal with
  77–8
'unstuck' helping you get 84

workshops 30

Young, J. 10n, 93